Cry Oneness

The spiritual adventures, miracles and poetry of a Retired Fire Rescue Lieutenant and Advanced Fire Safety Educator

Joseph Avalos

En Route Books and Media, LLC
5705 Rhodes Avenue
St. Louis, MO 63109

Cover Design by TJ Burdick
Cover Photo of the Holy Face by Joseph Avalos.
Vero Beach, Florida, December 18, 2008.

Copyright-free images within the book were selected from Wikimedia or taken by the author.

LCCN: 2018930611

ISBN-10: 0-9991143-6-0
ISBN-13: 978-0-9991143-6-0

DEDICATION

In memory of my beloved nephew Shawn, a "true friend to all".

CONTENTS

ACKNOWLEDGMENTS

I'd like to acknowledge the support of all my friends in recovery who loved me till I learned to love myself. I'd also like to thank the Little Flower, on whose Feast Day my birthday fell.

Introduction A

My name is Joe A.

I was spiritually dead, despite all the ***things*** I was doing with my life. I don't think there's a worse death that can happen to any human being. Now, I have a life beyond my dreams. Full of Miracles, Poetry, and Locutions. This is my first book.

This book won't necessarily be in chronological order. It is written in three sections:

Section One - My Story - What my life was like, what happened?, and what it's like now!

Section Two - Twelve experiences in my life that I consider Miracles.

Section Three - 65 Poems and locutions I've written or transcribed since 2007.

Section Two, my miracles section, contains

a photo I took in Vero Beach Florida, in 2008, while singing Josh Groban's song, "To where you are." It is also the cover photo of this book!

The story about this photo will be a story in itself. It is the most awesome GOD thing I've ever experienced. There will also be a photo with each miracle, poem, and locution that I feel matches the message of the miracle, poem, or locution.

I'll leave it up to you to decide if each writing is a poem or locution (a message from my higher power, whom I call the Holy Spirit).

I hope you enjoy this book! For more miracles, poems and locutions from myself and others, go to www.cryoneness.org today. Share your own story, your poems, songs, and miracles on links to our social media groups.

Visit me as well on my radio program, which runs every Wednesday night at 8:00 pm Eastern on wcatradio.com. You can find a year's worth of recorded shows posted there as well.

Let everyone know that our God is alive and well TODAY.

Introduction B

This is my First Formal Lay Witness – I call it "Joe's Salvation Story."

I told it to St Helen's Charismatic Prayer Group in Vero Beach, Florida, in 2007 on the Topic of Salvation as part of the 8-week Life in the Spirit course they were giving. My witness was on the topic of salvation.

So, here it is - "Joe's Salvation Story" – it begins: Something is wrong in the World.

There must be because here is how it affected me:

I was a Church-going frightened Catholic all my life. My life was a mess with alcohol and prescription drugs.

I agreed with the death penalty for capital crimes, and I approved of abortion, all in direct defiance with God's word.

I justified everything by thinking: "But all my friends did it!"

I justified everything this way: as long as someone I loved was doing worse than me, then I was ok. God would forgive me directly even without confession.

That is because God was my little slave. Anything I wanted he gave me. I spoke to him directly. Sometimes, I felt just like him, I'D LIE IN BED AT NIGHT PRAYING TO HIM ABOUT WHAT HE DID WRONG TODAY AND HOW HE COULD FIX IT TOMORROW.

I WENT TO CHURCH AND BELIEVED IN HIM. I DESERVED EVERYTHING I ASKED FOR.

As a result, I was in pain for fifty-three years, living in sin and desolation.

Despair, anxiety, and depression were my days and nights. TV was my God and my sedation.

Worldly things were my pleasure. I had lost all joys in my life.

I had everything in the world, but the world had taken me down! Good things I did with evil hidden motives.

Finally, I was sitting on the floor in my kitchen with God the Father and Satan, and I had a bottle of prescription sedatives on my lap.

TV didn't work anymore.

I had met Jesus in a hotel bathroom three weeks prior, but that just scared me more. I was ready to end my life. Jesus came and dialed 211, which in the northeast is a shortcut to all kinds of emergency services.

And that was the beginning of my new life with him, but I still didn't, know him. Before this, God the Father and the Church were where I placed my salvation. My focus was authority-based, not love-based. The father sent Jesus to save me. Praise Jesus!

The spiritual war in the world cannot be fought alone. Evil, particularly Satan, is too strong for us. We need spiritual tools to help Christ protect us.

After Christ saved me, I progressed slowly toward spiritual healing of my damaged soul. I repented of my sins, my drinking, my lust, my pride, my sloth, my everything. Jesus helped me every step of the way. Then, after a year, he took me to My Father's House in Moodus, CT, for more lessons.

I went to frequent masses and confessions, said rosaries, and did the Chaplet of Divine Mercy daily at 3:00 pm in commemoration of the hour of my best friend's crucifixion.

I purchased a daily bible at the National Shrine of Divine Mercy and have read it every day for the past year and a half.

I am saved, and Christ has made certain that I have all the daily weapons necessary to protect my new salvation.

I practice daily salvation with him. Here is how:

I wake up Praise his name and ask him to please keep me saved today – "Thy will not mine be done." I then ask him:

"Help me to keep accepting everything the Father places in my path, and help me help as many as I can by keeping a positive attitude in Christ."

I go to a 7 AM Mass and pray a 9 AM rosary, do a one-hour walk and meditation at 11:30, a daily spiritual 12-Step Program, and at 3PM, THE DIVINE MERCY CHAPLET. I stop everything and take a moment to venerate Him and thank him for dying for me.

Then, evening daily Bible readings and a gratitude list for the day entered into a personal journal.

I don't always get everything done, but Christ is the Center of My Life.

He surrounds me with friends of the same or similar type. I attend as many workshops and retreats as possible.

I volunteer for St. Helens, and I love my new life in Christ. My new found brother of three years. Life is GOOD if I walk with him.

Here is my bag of weapons:

- The Catholic Daily Bible Daily Rosary

- Daily Mass
- Hail Holy Queen
- Divine Mercy Chaplet (rosary Beads)

I live one day at a time.

WHATEVER IS WRONG WITH YOUR LIFE, CHRIST CAN FIX. PRAY AND LIVE LIKE THERE IS NO TOMORROW!!!

SECTION 1: MY STORY

Image Source: TheCulinaryGeek from Chicago, USA, 2010, Courtesy of Wikimedia.

"What my life was like,
what happened, what it's like now!"

"What my life was like, what happened, what it's like now!"

I was born in Stamford, Connecticut, in a city project. From a very early age, I was addicted to my own way of thinking. I grew up around a lot of drinking and always thought that drinking was stupid and that I would never do it when I grew up. Boy was I wrong!

I was critical of other people and extremely selfish. I exhibited all the characteristics that I now know are signs and symptoms of alcoholism. I was always self-centered and full of fear. I had asthma and a lazy eye. I felt different. At the age of 12, I almost died of pneumonia.

I was never satisfied doing anything a little bit at a time. I always had to have a lot of things going on at the same time. I was in extreme need of control. At age 12, my blood pressure was 200/100, and I was put on Valium 5 mg 3x a day after my first adult doctor gave me a physical. I was only 5'2" and weighed about 100 pounds soaking wet at the time.

Between the ages of 14 and 22, I was volunteering at a local Catholic hospital, teaching for the Red Cross, the American Heart Association, and the state emergency medical services. I was also a volunteer firefighter and ambulance driver. I thought that if I could please everyone in the world, I might feel better about myself.

I could never get enough of anything. I could never focus on first things first. I always had to be juggling a lot of balls in the air, all at once. I was addicted to chaos at a very young age. I loved managing other people's disasters, and I thought my life was in perfect control. I was extremely successful at other people's expense. I needed to heal other people. I was always right.

When I picked up my first beer with my friend Rob at age 22, I didn't have a chance. I got dizzy and had a panic attack, but I practiced real hard and overcame that problem. I finally had no fear and felt normal just like all those people I had thought were stupid drunks.

I had a great family but never felt like I belonged. I had a nagging feeling of emptiness. Within 2 years of starting to drink, I had the worst boating accident on Long Island Sound while drinking, and it almost killed two friends and myself. Two of us were rendered unconscious. I still have crooked teeth and scars from hitting the dashboard.

I was so upset that a couple of months later, at one of my annual drunken Halloween parties, I dressed up as a ghost. The drink of the night was “Sea Craft on the Rocks” (the name of my brand new boat that had a hole in the fiberglass hull big enough to crawl through).

My insane drinking persisted for 35 years fueled by a prescribed medication that quadrupled the effect of alcohol and detoxed me when I was not drinking. I became a bar room binge drinker. I accomplished a lot at work, but my off duty-life became a disaster. I started having a lot of sick leave caused by hangovers.

My longest relationship was 6 years. I never married. My relationships were just like my drinking - a series of one-night stands followed by unbelievable guilt and shame. I harmed my entire family and all my friends with my behavior.

The ambulance people and police to whom I taught EMS started having to come and give me rides to the emergency room. I had to go into hospital detox twice, and both times I signed myself out of a 30-day program against medical advice after only eight days.

One week, I'd be training for a marathon or running one, and the next week I'd be drinking myself unconscious and close to death or to another trip to the emergency room.

My drinking caused me to accept a disability pension at age 44. I was way too young to retire into full time drinking and feeling sorry for myself. But I did.

My 21-year career in one of the best jobs in the world was over. I had few friends left. During the first year of my retirement, I was so crazy I had seven W2s to file.

I stopped working completely and volunteered, while still drinking, to organize an international baseball event in my community. I recruited 6 division heads and 25 committee chairs with 750 volunteers and tightly managed everything for 4 years.

I was so hungover the day of the event's international trophy presentation that I almost fell over while presenting the trophy to the California champs. The division heads committee had tried to 12-step me the week before. I was totally out of my head. God bless them.

I went on a yoga retreat the week after the series at the Kripaula center in Lenox, Massachusetts, to try to calm down. I was standing in front of the Dali Lama's picture when I heard in my heart, "Don't let the lie you're living become the truth of who you are." I started yelling out loud at the picture, "Who do you think you are talking to Dali Lama? I don't even believe in you! I'm Catholic." I was a mess not having TV to watch, so I'm having a discussion with the Dali Lama's picture.

The next day, I decided to sit in on a yoga sharing circle. The counselor had all of us draw a picture of ourselves. I drew a picture of my face. When the instructor collected the drawings, she gasped and said, “Joe, I haven't seen anything like this in a long time.” “That good!” I replied. “No,” she said, “I haven't seen anything like this since I stopped counseling abused children two years ago. You are the only one in the group who didn't draw your whole body?”

I did a geographic change and moved to Naugatuck, Connecticut, in 2002 to get away from all the people who knew how messed up I was. When I left town, I was the only one in town who didn't think I had a drinking problem. I was determined to get a fresh start.

I know now that at this time in my life, I was acting like a 52-year-old baby, still codependent and living with my parents who were both ill. My emotional growth had stopped at age 13 when I started the valium and declined more at age 22 when I added alcohol.

I tried some controlled drinking, then became a dry drunk, taking care of my mother with Alzheimer's. That same year, I lost both my father, whom I cared for most of my life, from heart disease and my beautiful 18-year-old nephew six months later in a fatal car accident.

He died in a vehicle my mother gifted him, and it was registered in my name. I was her power of attorney. She was the only person in the world whom I thought still loved me and she now had Alzheimer's. So now the health-care expert finally had a disease he couldn't take care of. My self-centered fear rapidly turned into anger, then rage. How could God do this to poor me?

I became emotionally dead from suppressing my anger. My prayer to God at this time was that he would take mom out of her pain and let me learn to live before I died.

I moved us from a condo to a small home, and my sister and my 2-year-old niece moved in with us. Mom and her disease and me my disease became totally incompatible. Finally, I exploded in front of my mom and sister about how I couldn't do this anymore. My beautiful unselfish, saintly mom said, "I don't want to make you unhappy, Joey. If you feel that way, I'll go into the nursing home." So, my sister being so concerned about Mom's health and mine used the opportunity to get mom into the nursing home where she worked. THANK GOD!

After that, my anxiety, depression, guilt, and fear caused by my nephew's death, my dad's death, and my mom's being institutionalized became too much for me to bear.

I had just refilled a bottle of Valium. My three-bedroom house was empty again except for me. I thought everyone in my family hated me as much as I hated myself. I sat in the middle of the floor, frozen in fear, with the phone and the bottle of pills on my lap and a glass of water to take them with. I could not think of one single thing left to live for.

I was a supervisor in 911, so my pride wouldn't let me call for help. Finally, and I don't know why (God does), I decided to dial 211 and talk to someone before I took the bottle of pills. They knew I was in trouble and sent an ambulance.

I arrived at St. Mary's Hospital in Waterbury, Connecticut. I was admitted to the psych unit. They took me off the Valium and put me on 2 mg of Ativan twice a day, a mood stabilizer, antipsychotics, and antidepressants. I was a walking dead man. I had no emotions at all remaining.

I was diagnosed bipolar. After three weeks of great counseling and group therapy, I felt so much safer than I ever had in my life that I didn't want to go home. I asked the psychiatrist if I could stay there longer. He replied, “No, Joe, I can't let you stay here longer.” When I asked him why, he said, “Because if I do, you will become addicted to us, and you'll be in an institution for the rest of your life." He told me he'd put me in six weeks of intensive outpatient rehab on a weekday-daily basis. I accepted this.

Although I still felt like a zombie most of the time from the depression during this outpatient work, I was getting better a little bit of time, which never satisfied me. Midway through the outpatient treatment, my birthday was coming up on October 1, so I asked Dr. Perez if it would be alright if I had a glass of wine on my birthday because my family was taking me out to a restaurant in my home town for dinner. Dr. Perez replied, "Sure, with all the shit you're on, a little wine won't hurt you."

So off I go to Stamford for my 55th birthday. I was looking forward to that glass of wine a lot more than I was looking forward to seeing my family in the condition I was in. However, when they brought me that glass of wine I had a moment of clarity. I took one sip, put it down, and realized I couldn't do this anymore. This was my last drink.

It has been 12 years now, and that's a miracle! This was the beginning of my physical healing, to be free of alcohol. Until I did this, nothing else good could happen. This was October 1, 2004.

I'm back now in outpatient, and it's Thanksgiving Day, 2004. The day of the discharge. We're having Thanksgiving dinner and final instructions. The Irish nurse practitioner, whom I loved because she gave me all of my pills, told us, “I want you all to take out a piece of paper. On one side of the paper write down everything you used to do that made you happy in your past life, and on the other side of the paper write down everything you're doing now for your recovery, to get those things back.”

I thought hard and stressed. I was so depressed still that I couldn't think of one thing in my life that I ever enjoyed. My mind was too negative to think of anything positive. I was still wired in complete reverse. But on that right side of the piece of paper, I lied and said I would go to Alcoholics Anonymous meetings.

When I handed the paper in to the nurse, she looked at me like I was lying. I said to her, “You know I lied. I didn't go to AA.” She said, “I know, but if you hurry down the hill out front you can catch the noon meeting right now.” I listened to her and walked down the hill.

On arrival, I saw a man outside smoking a cigarette. I said to myself, “That's it. I don't smoke.” As I started to turn around, the man called to me, “Where are you going?” I said, “I don't know. I don't think I belong here. I'm on fluvoxamine 25 mg twice a day for depression.”

He looked me in the eyes, took a puff on his cigarette, extended his hand, and said, “I'm on fluvoxamine 250 mg twice a day. Welcome to AA my friend!”

I've been going to AA meetings, once a day, ever since!

So, I had my last drink on October 1, 2004, and I had my first AA meeting on Thanksgiving day 2004, and I celebrated 90 meetings in 90 days on New Year's Day.

God wanted to make sure I remembered all the most important dates in my new life.

What about now? Well, I have a bunch of great friends in Alcoholics Anonymous. I go to meetings every day. I give back what I was so freely given. I love my life and everyone in it. Even the ones I don't like that much. I practice love and service. I go to a lot of spiritual retreats, and I share the miracles that I receive.

I now see God’s hands in my life, by looking backwards and “connecting the dots” through spiritual eyes after getting sober in 2004.

Through the grace of God and the fellowship of AA, I celebrated 13 years of sobriety this October 1st. God willing, I will continue.

I currently have a life beyond my wildest dreams, and the miracles and poetry you will be reading about are still happening today as I write.

SECTION 2: MY MIRACLES

Cover Photo of the Holy Face by Joseph Avalos.
Vero Beach, Florida, December 18, 2008.

DIVINE MERCY EXPERIENCE 1995

Photo of the National Shrine of Divine Mercy Courtesy of Wikipedia. Photographer, John Phelan, December 19, 1992.

Looking backwards, connecting the dots, the first major spiritual experience I had in my life was at the Divine Mercy Chapel at the National Shrine of Divine Mercy in Stockbridge, Massachusetts, in 1995. Here's what happened.

I was driving home from my yoga retreat in Lenox, Massachusetts, on Route 7, in Connecticut. I had been staying there for a week, eating vegetarian food and practicing hot Vanesa yoga for seven days. I lost 5 pounds. I was in an amazing spiritual place.

When I was driving through Stockbridge near the Red Lion Inn, I noticed a very small sign on a post that said "Divine Mercy Shrine." I almost stopped because I had started doing the Divine Mercy Chaplet in 1993 after seeing it on television on EWTN.

I had also read the *Diary of Saint Faustina*, which is an autobiography written by a Polish nun who was in constant communication with Jesus and founded the Divine Mercy devotion.

However, I wound up deciding not to stop there because I felt good enough without doing that. I said to myself, “I’ll drive back some other day.”

Seven miles later, I stopped on Route 7 to get some ice cream. I had to go the bathroom there, and when I sat down, there was a Bible right next to me on the counter in the bathroom. I opened randomly to a page and the phrase I read made me believe I had to go back to the Shrine of Divine Mercy.

When I got back to the Divine Mercy Shrine sign, I drove up Eden Hill and entered the beautiful National Chapel of Divine Mercy.

I stood there in awe. I felt the same way I did when I was seven years old when I received my first communion. Standing there, my whole body began to feel abnormally heavy, weighted, and grounded. Any anxiety I had left in my body was gone. I felt a peace that surpassed all understanding. I stood motionless as if glued to the floor in a trance looking at the Divine Mercy image above the altar.

I went to the Divine Mercy gift shop and picked up a set of rosary beads and the daily Catholic Bible.

From that day on, each day till the present time, I've been doing the Chaplet of Divine Mercy on rosary beads. These days, I sing it when nobody can hear me.

According to Saint Faustina, Jesus told her

that anybody who prayed this chaplet even once was guaranteed a personal audience before HIM at the time of their death. I got one, a personal visit, before I died, which is documented in the next chapter, "Dark Night of the Spirit."

This devotion didn't stop anything bad from happening to me, including my breakdown, but I'm pretty sure that if I wasn't doing this devotion for 10 years before my breakdown, I would probably have been dead instead of broken.

I never saw this as a miracle until several years after I got sober. These days, everything is a miracle in my eyes. My first breath every day is a miracle. Grass growing is a miracle. And especially my sobriety is a miracle.

In the next witness, I'll discuss a very large personal miracle at the Holiday Inn in downtown Waterbury, which included a private revelation from Jesus. You be the judge after reading my witness.

Lt. Joe Avalos, Stamford Fire Rescue. Circa late 1990s.

DARK NIGHT OF THE SPIRIT 2004

Vitral em Igreja Santa Efigenia, Courtesy of Wikimedia.
September 6, 2014.

This witness happened about two months before my near suicide attempt. My sister was having some difficulties and came to live with me. We were both having emotional difficulties after the death of my nephew in the car accident.

We were staying in the Holiday Inn in downtown Waterbury. We had just gotten back from Vero Beach, Florida, where we went to get some relief from our chaos.

My sister and my god-daughter had joined me at the Holiday Inn in Waterbury after I picked them up from the airport. They stayed in Vero Beach longer than I had.

We went to bed late. I was extremely tired and emotionally dead. There was nothing left of me. I wasn't feeling well at all.

I was restless and couldn't get to sleep. I dozed off and woke back up again. I looked out the hotel window, to my left, and saw a large illuminated cross. I now know that's the cross at the "Holy Land" in Waterbury, but at the time, I didn't know this.

I looked over at my sister and my niece on the other bed. My two-year-old niece and sister were asleep but hugging each other close. Their position for some reason reminded me of the Virgin Mary holding the child Jesus, protecting him from the world.

Then, I felt a strange spiritual presence in the room. I felt like somebody was massaging me, but they were using my own hands. It felt better than it ever felt when I massaged myself. I heard a very soft inner voice telling me that everything will be alright.

It scared me a little bit, so I got up in my jockey shorts and walked over to look in the large mirror on the dresser of the hotel room.

Instead of seeing myself, in human form, I

saw myself in a glowing spiritual form. I felt like I was in a trance, so I went into the bathroom to take a shower. For some reason, instead of getting into the shower, I got into a yoga pose called "tree" in front of the bathroom sink.

Then things got crazy. I perceived a strong inner voice, similar to the voice I heard in front of the Dali Lama's picture at the Kripala Yoga Center. The voice said, "I am the Alpha and the Omega." I started laughing at the voice. That didn't seem like the right thing to do. I went into like a body spasm, and words and thoughts, but not really words and thoughts, more like beams of light and wind, started to go in and out of me.

Then, I heard the voice again. It said, "Are you willing to die for them?" I started weeping uncontrollably. My whole body was trembling. I said, "You are God the Father, and you're talking to me?"

I got a hold of myself and said, "You mean, die for my sister and niece?" The voice said no.

Then I went through a bunch of exercises, but not really exercises, and I heard, "The line between good and evil is so thin as to be invisible."

Then the voice said, "My mother is the key to your salvation. You will work with the Betia, in the place between heaven and earth, to save souls." (Years later, I looked up Betia and discovered that it's a Hebrew girl's name meaning, "woman of God.")

Now, I suddenly became aware of knocking at the bathroom door. I couldn't answer the door. I was in an extreme case of what I know now to be Ecstasy, in total awe, of God.

Suddenly, two paramedics entered the bathroom. I couldn't respond to them verbally. I was slayed in the spirit. They threatened to put a Foley catheter in me if I didn't move. Without speaking, I calmly laid down on their stretcher. They brought me quietly to St. Mary's hospital in the ambulance. I was plastered in the Spirit.

My sister talked to me. And I talked to her. I told her I never felt better. In fact, I never felt more peace in my lifetime than I did laying there in the hallway on the stretcher. I had full knowledge that my God loves me and had taken time out to make a personal visit. Maybe as the result of 10 years of bible reading and reciting the Divine Mercy Chaplet, I'm thinking now.

I allowed to myself to sign myself into the psych unit at the request of my sister.

I thought I was only in the bathroom in Waterbury for about two or three minutes, but she told me I was in there for two hours. That means that for two hours I was in an extremely difficult yoga position called tree, which looks just like the position of Christ on the cross. If you're a yoga person, try getting in the position called tree and holding that position for two hours. On second thought, don't even try!

I was extremely calm as I entered the psych unit at St Mary's Hospital, but as soon as they closed the doors, I when into a total panic, a deep fear that I would lose this feeling of ecstasy that had entered my body.

I jumped out of the wheelchair and squirmed around the floor like a snake trying to escape from them. Screaming for Jesus. Finally, they restrained me on the floor and shot me up with Thorazine.

I woke up the next morning in four point restraints. I felt very calm. I looked to my right and saw a very unhappy nurse with an angry look on her face. She had been sitting there all night, she said.

I told her I was alright. She removed the restraints, and I walked around the unit, wrapped in a white sheet only.

One of the nurses came up to me while I was walking around slowly, wrapped in this white sheet, and asked me if I would like to receive ashes as it was Ash Wednesday and a priest was standing at the entry door to the unit with ashes. This meant that the evening all this happened to me was Shrove Tuesday 2004, the Feast of the Holy Face of Jesus.

The psychiatrist came in to speak with me. I now had my full composure back. I explained fully what happened the night before. I told him I was okay now, and that it was just an amazing spiritual experience.

He looked at me and said, "I wish we had a video tape of what you did last night. You spent all night screaming and hollering for Jesus, even after we gave you the medication." I knew through my EMS training that Thorazine could knock out a horse. I said, "I don't remember that but I fully believe it."

I spent the next three days convincing the psychiatrist to discharge me, which he did, and as you have already read, later I would be readmitted after my near suicidal episode with the bottle of Valium.

For many years in sobriety, I thought this witness was just insanity. But the future events I will describe in this book proved to me, and hopefully will convince you, that this was my first invitation from God, to share His wounds and life with me.

God will do anything to get even one sinner back, physically, mentally, and spiritually. He wants all of us, body, mind, and spirit, to be fearless servants.

GIFT OF TONGUES 2006

Acts 2, Courtesy of Wikimedia

At one of my many trips to My Father's House in Moodus, Connecticut, I met Bob Olson, a lay evangelist, and his wife.

They were great people and had a lot of training in spiritual warfare.

Some of it was through Neal Lazano's heart of the father unbound ministries. After hearing my stories about some of my miracles and locutions, they strongly advised me to take an eight-week Life in the Spirit course so that I could develop better powers of discernment of spirits.

They told me the next course was in New Haven. I trusted them and signed up.

It was an eight-week course based on scripture and designed at the end to re-baptize the attendee in the Holy Spirit .

The course leaders prayed over people at the end and requested the seven gifts of the Spirit be activated in the attendees.

I thoroughly enjoyed the course but wasn't sure if anything would really happen to me after it.

One day, weeks later, I was at a friend's house in Stamford, Connecticut, with my 5-year-old goddaughter, Michele, and their grandson, Christopher, who were wrestling .

I was afraid they would hurt one another, and when I went to holler something at them in English, loud words came out in a language I didn't know instead.

Both 5-year-olds froze in action immediately and looked at me with such bright, wide eyes that I thought they would pop out. They never stopped doing anything that quickly when asked before.

It was like they and all time had frozen instantly. For seconds, all reference to time was suspended by some force we didn't understand.

Finally, they broke the silence by laughing and shouting in unison with great awe. "Do it again, Uncle Joe."

I, too, being in shock replied.

“I can't. I don't even know what I just said.”

They laughed hysterically and resumed wrestling, and I stood still trying to figure out who or what had just happened to us.

Was I going insane? Then, it hit me. I had just received the gift of tongues as promised by Bob and his wife, the Life in the Spirit instructors at Saint Brenden’s in New Haven.

I called Bob Olson in awe, and he said, “Just accept the gift and keep practicing.”

I said "practice what? This is just like my poems. I don't have a clue as to how to do it again.” He said just babble like a baby and the Spirit will come alive in you and speak again through you. You will have nothing to do with it. It's total surrender to the Spirit.

I saw him again at a retreat, and he asked me how it felt to speak in tongues. I said it's like a dose of joyful exhaustion, like the endorphin feeling I felt in 1995 after running a marathon.

He agreed.

What a great feeling you get when you surrender your all to God, and His Spirit starts speaking back to God in words that come from your heart that you don’t even understand. Unless you have the gift of translations of tongue , which I don't. YET. WITH GOD ALL THINGS ARE POSSIBLE.

GIFT OF LOCUTIONS 2007

In 2007, my next major God moment occurred. I moved to Vero Beach, Florida, thinking I would retire there on my pension alone. The tremendous change gave me an emotional relapse to overcome. My sobriety was very unstable. I went to a lot of meetings and was then on a "pink cloud."

I prayed for a woman to come into my life, and the next day Rita showed up at St. Helens Church in the pew behind me. We became great friends. We rode around Vero Beach in her red convertible with the top down. I got back on the spiritual beam. She was in the same Life in the Spirit program I had taken at St Brenden's in New Haven. We hit it off great. She had many miracles in her life like me. That was a miracle in itself, but not as large as the one I'll share now.

I was at a 12-step meeting in Vero Beach, and a man sat down beside me with some poetry he used to read at nursing homes as service work. I looked at his poems, and for some strange reason I asked God if I could write poetry.

The phrase "Be careful what you pray for" took a new meaning for me. Within seconds I heard thoughts that I knew were not mine. So I grabbed a date book I had in my pocket (I still have it saved as precious) and wrote down the words that seemed to come a line at a time. As fast as I could write these, two stanzas flew out:

Through the ancient dessert trounced the

silent winds of time. Decades screaming for the light.
Caressing dreams of wandering souls.
Voices whispering in the sands of weathered beaches, on the shorelines of mankind.
Passionate trails of blighted past. Leading to the endless light.
Frightened not the faithful servants. Choosing good, instead of evil.
The fight is never all for naught. Cry Oneness to the Lord. Unity WILL overcome.

I was struck in awe. I didn't even know what these verses meant, let alone what naught meant, or that sands in beaches had voices.

I drove people crazy for weeks. I was in the rooms asking everyone what this was and if it was a poem. I never wrote anything other than technical instructions and EMS course outlines prior to this event. Poetry was all Greek to me. But then I thought this is amazing how fast God answers prayers. I prayed for a woman friend and got one the day after; I asked if I could write poetry and two seconds later I wrote a poem?

All this started to scare me, so I went to St. John of the Cross Church and asked the priest what this thing I wrote was, as I didn't believe anyone who said this was a poem.

So this became my first meeting with Fr. John Jude. He read my writing and quickly told me. “It’s not a poem, Joe, it’s a locution, a message from God’s spirit. It comes from your heart not your mind, and your locution is about man’s Salvation. I want to tell you something else: Today at our church, in the hall, Ralph Martin is here from EWTN giving a talk on his new book, *The Fulfillment of All Our Desires*. His book coincidently is on the same topic as your locution, Salvation. There is a charge for this program, but you can attend for free on me.”

Well, there you have it. My miracle of poetry and locutions. Even though I was so horrible in writing in high school that I barely graduated, and firefighters aren't likely to write poetry, here I am a poet receiving messages from God’s spirit.

SAN DIEGO MIRACLE 2007

This was the first of two miracles I experienced involving God using photographs to prove that He, His Mother, and his army of saints were real. First just to review what He had done to convert men already.

1 He gave me my first locution in Lenox mass at the Kripala Yoga center by

speaking to me through the Dali Lama's picture.

2 He made a very scary personal appearance for me at the Holiday Inn in Waterbury, Connecticut, where He introduced Himself as the Alpha and the Omega and told me his Mother was the key to my salvation.

3 He saved me from killing myself with a bottle of Valium by getting me to dial 211.

4 He gave me all the pain I needed to get into AA. Saving my Life and my mind.

5 Through Bob Olson, He got me to take the Life in the Spirit program.

6 He gave me the woman I prayed for.

7 He gave me the gift of Locutions and Poetry.

And He wasn't finished. Within a month, I had six or seven new poems including "Communion with a Friend," which was a locution that came out of me as a song while I was working at Miracle Mile as a security guard. I sang it out loud, uncontrollably, after telling Him the poems I was writing were scaring me. Here is what I sang spontaneously.

"Communion with a Friend"

One sip of wine.
One bread in our time. One hope for mankind.
Who do you go to when dark days are near? Now that the word of your day is fear.
Remember my mercy is ALWAYS near. Revealed long ago by the spirit of Love.
The Lamb is alive and dancing a waltz, as the era of mercy follows His cross. So wake up, and listen my kind-hearted friends,
Mercy yields forgiveness but judgements offend. So just stay with Him in your sacred place.
Just pray for mercy and receive His grace.
For His heart is as soft as the breath of an angel. He whispers His message in the still of His might. Come and receive Him in the presence of light.
Come, love your Jesus.
Come, give up your Fight.

Why? Because, I guess, whatever you tell Him you're afraid of, He'll get you over it by giving it to you until the fear is replace by faith. That's what I think now.

While in Vero Beach, I frequently went to

the Barefoot Cafe. The couple there were very spiritual. I asked them why all these things were happening to me, and I believe God spoke this through them. “Because, Joe, your name should be Thomas. He’s showing you His wounds because He will do anything to save a poor sinner.”

Well, that’s true in my mind now. That's a little reminder of what already happened. Now on to “My Miracle in San Diego” while I was serving with the National Red Cross disaster response team, RNT division, at Red Cross Headquarters.

After serving for three weeks at the wild fires in 2007, the RNT division got together for a farewell dinner at The Popes Place restaurant in San Diego. I was walking around the restaurant looking at all the religious photos on the wall before I returned to the rental car that was packed, locked, and loaded for the airport in the AM.

I was very strongly drawn to one of the

photos on the wall of a beautiful young lady with a welcoming smile. It was almost as if the picture was alive and calling me. Just another crazy mystical experience, I said to myself.

When I got into my car to leave, there was a long-stemmed rose on the front console between the front seats. I said, "That's odd. I thought I locked the car. One of my friends must be playing a joke on me." I went about my business and flew home to my place in Vero Beach.

St. Therese de Lisieux, Photo by Author.

My friend Rita met me on my condo balcony. I was so curious about the photo at the Popes Place, and I knew she knew a lot more about Saints than I did. I showed her the picture I took of the photo that attracted me on the wall.

She said very enthusiastically. That's Saint Theresa, the Little Flower. You didn't happen to get any Roses out there, did you? Saint Theresa showers people on earth with Roses.

Not really believing dead Saints can do anything at this phase of my recovery, I went to an AA meeting and told the first man I saw what happened to me and how unbelievably crazy it sounded, and how I was concerned about Rita's mental health. He quickly responded to me: "Oh, Saint Theresa got you, too!"

After my heart almost fluttered out of my chest, I NOW started to believe in dead saints serving people on earth. Especially my favorite, Saint Theresa of the Child Jesus and the Holy Face, AKA the "Little Mama." The big mama would be Mother Mary, and neither one of them were finished with poor little scared Joe just yet. On now to the Holy Face Miracle.

HOLY FACE MIRACLE 2007

Less than a month after my encounter with Saint Theresa of the Holy Face, I was back in Vero Beach after a trip home to Stamford to see my sick mom in the Smith House skilled nursing home. I drove my car up to Stamford and came back on the auto train because I was tired of driving and love trains.

I wound up sitting next to an older man and started talking about my experiences and how I thought that I was too old at 58 for this kind of stuff to be happening.

He laughed and said he was 90 and just started taking piano lessons. He also, after viewing a couple of my poems, said my poetry reminded him of Josh Groban's songs especially one called "Up to where you are," which was written by an Irish poet.

Not being too patient I immediately googled the song and listen to it and fell in love with it. Especially since I found out it was used for grief support in California because the verses sound like they are a tribute to relatives that have passed. I decided to practice singing it.

I try real hard to sing songs I love. Even though I'm not fond of how I sound, Rita told me, "Don't worry. Singing is great for the soul. Don't ever let anyone say you don't sound good."

So I practiced singing this song at the bank of the Indian River and was happy with the way I sang it, and I told the Lord, "I'd rather sing than get more poems because they are still scaring me. Please don't give me any more poems."

Being sure He would listen this time, I joyfully took 10 shots of the beautiful sunset with my iPhone while singing the following words:

Who can say for certain, maybe you're still here,
I feel you all around me, your memories so clear,
Deep in the stillness, I can hear you speak,
You're still an inspiration, can it be, that you are mine forever love, and you are watching me from up above,
Fly me up to where you are, beyond the distant star,
I wish for just tonight to see you smile.

After finishing the song, which is a tribute to dead Irish relatives, I looked at the ten photos. One had a strange-looking face in it, and was beyond a star, and NOT smiling.

Off I ran to St John of the cross again to see Fr. John Jude, in a panic. After telling the Lord his poems are scaring me, now I have a scary Face.

Fr. John Jude pointed to a photo on his office wall. It was Veronica's veil - THE HOLY FACE blood soaked imprint left on the scarf of St. Veronica after she wiped off Jesus's Face when he was carrying the cross. "So, you're being led by the Lord to a Holy Face Devotion," said Father John Jude calmly. The face in your photo is the Shroud Face of Jesus.

Now, the reason Fr. John Jude was calm. He took the name of St. Jude. St. Jude the Apostle was entrusted to carry the folded shroud of Turin (burial cloth of Jesus) with him. In the days of the early Church, it is believed by many that they celebrated mass on the Shroud. It has both wine stains and blood stains on it according to scientists who examined the Holy Shroud with permission from the pope. I knew absolutely nothing about St. Jude, the Shroud of Turin, Veronica's veil or anything about the Holy Face at the time of this new miracle in my life.

But I do know this. Three years later, I was researching a Holy Face prayer group for my church. I was working security at a factory next to the Crab Shell Restaurant in Stamford, having moved back to Connecticut a year prior.

I googled Holy Face of Jesus and came to a site called Confraternities of Passionists, International Association of the Holy Face. Donald Nohls was President. It was 8:00 at night on a weekday, but I was moved to call and leave a message. A man answered the phone on two rings saying hello. Surprised anyone answered this late, I said with surprise, "Whose This?" He said, "This is Don Nohls!" I said, "Oh, Ok, I want to start a prayer group dedicated to the Holy Face. Can you give me some information to give to my Pastor?" He said, "Where are you?" I said, "What does that have to do with anything? I'm working a security job near the crab shell restaurant in the south end of Stamford." He said, "I'm on I95, driving through Stamford. I have just finished a Shroud of Turin presentation in Connecticut and am heading back to Queens. I have a Vatican-authorized copy of the Shroud of Turin in a trailer behind my car. Give me the address. I'll see you in a couple of minutes."

One month after our meeting, I was helping Don, the Apostle of the Holy Shroud and Lay-sworn Passionist give two sets of presentations at St John's Basilica in Stamford to about 600 people.

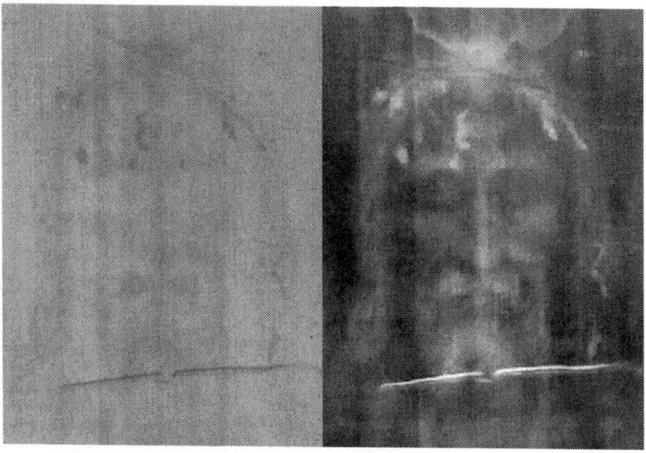

Shroud of Turin, Cathedral of Saint John the Baptist
Turin, Italy, Courtesy of Wikimedia

Less than a year later, I joined the confraternity and took vows as a Lay Passionist at the Jamaica Queens Passionists Monastery of the Immaculate Conception. Eight years later, I consecrated my life to Mary on the Feast of the Immaculate Conception at St Margaret's Church in Danbury, which was on the first day of the Year of Mercy as proclaimed by Pope Frances. This is what happens when it's the Spirit moving us instead of us moving ourselves.

GALDINO'S MIRACLE 2008

Image courtesy of Galdino Velasco.

It's now about 2008 or 9. Rita and I are engaged and traveling a lot together. Rita has the Gift of Healing and has been to Medjugorie where Mother Mary has appeared. She has a handkerchief from there that she carries with her, which was soaked with the water that flows out of the knee of a statue of Jesus – reported to be a miracle in Medjugorie.

At this time, she was helping me promote the website I had built called cryoneness.com for the purpose of lay evangelizing because of all the things that were happening to me. But I decided lay evangelizing was too much for my 4 years of sobriety to handle. We did a cryoneness media launch at my friend Galdino's Mexican Restaurant. No media showed up, but some old friends did.

When I introduced Rita to Galdino and shook his hand, I saw that he didn't look good. His hands were cold. He goes to kidney dialysis twice a week, so I just let it go for then after asking Rita to pray for him. Rita and I headed up to a weekend retreat at My Father's House in Moodus, Connecticut, to see my friend, Fr. Bill McCarthy. Fr. Tom Forest was there, giving a retreat.

Fr. Tom Forest was a confessor for Mother Theresa, who is another saint I petition every day nowadays. I was anxious to talk to Fr. Tom after his talk, to see if he thought my locutions were from God. He said, "Joe, they are definitely the Word of God, but now you have to discern what the Lord wants you to do with them. He will let you know. I can't interfere."

I was a little upset Fr. Tom didn't tell me what to do. Fr. Tom and the 30 people at the retreat all sat down to eat and share stories.

Then, another very scary spiritual thing happened. I looked at Rita. It was about 6:30Pm, and I saw that both her arms from her elbows down to her hands looked black like a corpse. I said, “Rita, what’s wrong with your arms.” She looked at her arms and calmly said, “Oh, I don’t know.” I said, “I think we should take you to the ER.” She kept eating and calmly said, “Oh, no, I’m probably just carrying something for someone I’m praying for.” I gasped, OK. In about an hour her arm returned to normal color. She said, “See, I told you.” I said, “Who do you think you were carrying something for?” She said, “I don't know but eventually we will find out.”

The next day I called TACO GUADALAJARA to talk to Galdino to see how my friend was feeling, and his son Johnny answered the phone. I said, “Johnny, is your Dad there?” He said, “No, you didn't hear?” I said, “Hear what?” He replied, “My Dad had a heart attack last night at about 6:30. He almost died in the ER. He was real bad for an hour. They put stents in, but then he got better.” I told Rita, and she said, “That was what I was carrying.”

The time he was critical matched exactly the time Rita's arms were black.

Galdino recovered completely. It took me a lot longer recovering enough spiritually to understand how prayer warriors like Rita carry illness for the people they pray for. I was afraid to pray for anyone for a while after this miracle.

CAPE COD MIRACLE

A little more about Rita to set the creditability for this miracle. Rita was a widow. She always wore a shorter dress, not to be sexy, but because she had a large scar on her right outer leg between her dress line and her knee. I once asked her why she didn't wear a longer dress to cover the large scar. She explained gracefully, “It’s my witness.” I asked, “What do you mean?” She then shared her witness with me as she had with many other doubters.

She, her husband, and her husband’s friend were biking one day in Vero. An out of control car hit all three of them. Her husband and his best friend were killed. Rita survived but was face down, her head in water and not breathing when the medics arrived. In her words, she was in heaven before Jesus while dead, and she told Him, “I want to stay here in heaven with my husband.” Jesus told her she couldn't and that he needed her to help him on earth.

After recovering from her very severe injuries, she became in charge of training the catechumens at St. Helens Church in Vero

Beach. She had 39 years in the spirit when we were dating. Her faith made my experiences look like nothing. What a great, courageous disciple she is.

So, off we went on another journey together to meet her family in Cape Cod. We were planning to get married soon. It never happened because of a problem with my mom's health in Connecticut, and I had to separate and return to Stamford. I still miss her, but it was a tough split up.

While in Cape Cod, we wound up going to Mass at the Church where the Kennedys married. There was an AA meeting downstairs followed by mass upstairs. Rita stayed in the Church while I went to the one-hour meeting. She was sitting in a pew right next to a beautiful statue of Our Lady of Medjugorie.

I returned for Mass after the meeting. Just before Mass began, a lady in the pew in front of us got very ill looking, and I walked over to help because I was still an EMT and had taught EMS for the Fire Department before retiring.

The Lady appeared to be having a heart problem, so I identified myself as having medical training. She told me it was alright to take her pulse. As soon as I started to take her pulse, she started turning blue and dry heaving like a heart patient. I then lost the pulse I had on her, but for some strange reason, instead of starting CPR immediately, I hesitated and asked the two ladies behind her to pray hard for her.

Rita had her cloth from Medjugorie and was praying too, but I defaulted to my EMT persona and started to grab the lady to put her down on the pew and start CPR. But as soon as I put my hand on her chest to start compressions she regained consciousness - returned to full normal color and was able to walk by the time the ambulance got there.

Was she healed by prayer to our Lady of Medjugorie, influenced by a miraculous handkerchief and raised from the dead, or was it a medical phenomenon?

I know what Rita and I and those three prayer warriors thought, but you decide for yourselves.

PRO-LIFE MARCH 2010

Courtesy of Wikimedia, Photographer James McNellis from Washington, DC. This photo taken on January 27, 2017.

I experienced a couple of miraculous events in this chapter. At this time in my life, I was active with the Holy Name group at St. John's Basilica in Stamford, Connecticut. They had a bus trip going to the pro-life march in Washington, DC.

I was hesitant about going because it was my last day on 2 milligrams of Valium twice a day. I had been on this medication since age 13, when I suffered frequently from panic attacks, but I decided to place my trust in Jesus and walk through the fear.

This wound up being the day I took my last dose and conquered my 53-year addiction to Valium. That was the first and largest miracle of this spiritual day trip in support of Life.

When the bus dropped us off at this awesome event, I began trying to locate Fr. Bill McCarthy's group from Moodus, Connecticut. I thought it might be impossible in this crowd, but I believed in miracles at this point in my life, so I walked up to a priest who was talking to a nice woman and her son and asked him if by any strange chance he had seen Fr. Bill McCarthy from My Father's House in Moodus. I was shocked when he pointed over to a flag about 50 yards away and said, "Yes, he's right over there."

Now at this point in my life, any time I saw a priest, I either asked them to tell me if they thought my locutions were God speaking to me or if the photo I took in Vero Beach contained the Face of Jesus. So I pulled out my iPhone and asked the priest if the photo I took 2 years ago contained the shroud face of Jesus. He took one look at my photo and said, "Where did you get that picture?" I said, "What do you mean? I took that photo." He said, "That's impossible. I have that photo as the screen saver on my computer."

Someone he knew must have sent him a copy from Vero Beach, I thought. I had given out hundreds of copies of this picture with the holy face in Vero Beach two years earlier.

So, then he passed the photo to the lady he was talking to and asked her if she saw anything? She said, "Oh, my God. I see the face of Jesus!" Then she passed the picture to her 12-year-old son, and he said, "I don't see Jesus's face, but I see Our Lady of Guadalupe in the water under the sunset."

So, it was my turn to say, "Oh, my God!" after I looked at the picture. When the boy showed me where in the picture our Lady was, I saw her, too, for the first time. I had only seen Jesus before that. Now, I see both, and it was plain to me that that beam of light is Mary pointing. (Take another look at the book cover. Do you see it?)

Our Lady of Guadalupe Shrine, Mexico. Photo by Author.

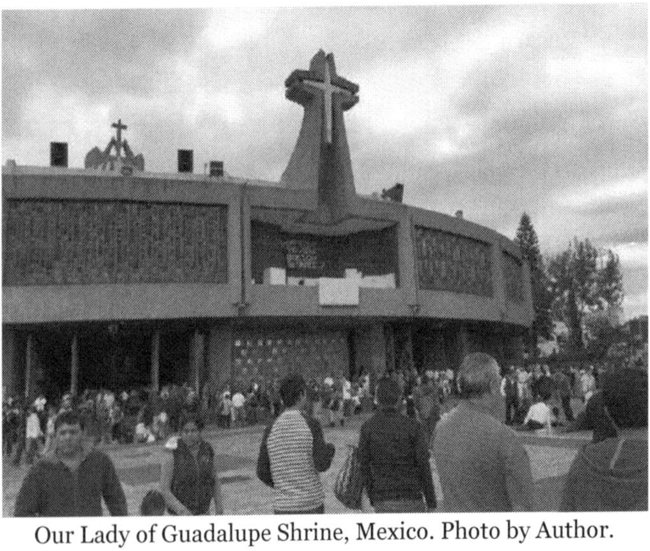

Our Lady of Guadalupe Shrine, Mexico. Photo by Author.

LET THE MUSIC BEGIN

Courtesy of Wikimedia.

While I was in Vero Beach, after I had written my first five poems, I had showed them to a lot of friends in my 12-step groups. One man who lived right on the water and used to say the dolphins spoke to him told me my poems were beautiful and were like lines in a song and that I should put music to them.

I said, “It’s crazy enough writing these poems. I don't have a clue how to write music. That will NEVER happen.” He laughed and said, "It will come to you someday." I laughed at him and left thinking he was crazy, but a great guy. I took his number and left.

Two years later, I was in Stamford at the Smith House with my mom. There was a charismatic guitar player there doing the music at mass. She's now a good friend, but I didn't know her then.

So, for some reason, the thought came into my mind, "Why don't you ask her to write music to your poems?" So I did. She looked at me with spiritually intense eyes and said, "I could, but I won't!" I thought, "How rude." But then she said, "I won't because you already have the music to your poem." I said, "You mean that tune I used to hum every time a jogged on the beach in Vero Beach is the music for my poem?" She said, "Yes, that's the music for your poem 'Cry Salvation.'"

A week later I began going to charismatic prayer group meetings with Gail at St. John's in Darien, Connecticut, every week and Gail gave me the sheet music for my first two poems, "Cry Oneness" and "A Miracle in Time," which are now the titles on two of my poems I had the music for at the date of this new God moment.

Being all excited, I called the friend in Vero Beach who had given me the idea to have music even though I hadn't seen him since I left. Unfortunately, his wife sadly informed me, "I'm so sorry. He passed away yesterday." Life is always so Good and Bad. God bless him.

DEATH OF MY SAINT

Courtesy of Wikimedia. Edvard Munch, The Dead Mother and Her Child, Between 1897 and 1899

Talking about life being so Good and Bad, the next miracle definitely proved this. This is why I moved back to Stamford, to be near my mom in her last days. She had been in hospice for 2 weeks and was in a coma and off all life supporting treatments because of her end stage Alzheimer's.

She was and is the most important person in my Life. I had taken over her rosary devotion ever since my miracle at the Divine Mercy Shrine in Stockbridge. She was supposed to be gone in two days, but she was always a fighter.

I was home in bed at 11 PM, and I only lived a mile from the Smith House Nursing Home. I had a thought at that moment that I should go to the Smith House to see mom.

I thought mom may have passed, but when I got there she was still suffering and fighting death. Her oxygen level was still 100%. I told her, "Mom, it's ok you can let go," but her oxygen stayed at 100%.

Then IT hit me like a ton of bricks, what might be wrong. I knelt beside her, doing a rosary.

Months ago, I told my 12-step sponsor, John, about a serious thing that happened with me. I had a gun to my head one night when I was drunk in front of my parents, blaming them for causing my drinking problems. It was one of those things I had stuffed away, and it had just been revealed to me 6 months prior.

My sponsor had told me that I needed to write an amends to my father who had already passed and to make a direct amends to my mother.

I told him I couldn't do that with my mom because it might make her dementia worse.

Now, kneeling at mom's side, for some reason, I knew I had to say something to her even though she was in a coma. While still on my knees, I said, "Mom, I'm so very sorry about what I said to you and dad that night when I was drunk, accusing you of causing my drinking problem and threatening to kill myself. Can you forgive me?"

Immediately, she took a deep sigh, and went into something called chain stoke breathing, and her oxygen level dropped to 40% from 100 in seconds.

I called the nurse and my sister at home. My sister arrived in minutes, before mom's heart stopped. We both laid beside mom, praying the rosary until mom's heart finally stopped—just fifteen minutes after I made my amends.

I believe my beloved mom was only hanging on to be able to have me ask for forgiveness before she passed, so she could forgive me before she died.

So, I thought to myself, unconscious people are much closer to God than conscious ones.

MIRACLE ON 33RD STREET

Courtesy of Wikimedia. Immaculee Uwanyiligira.
Photographer: TEDx Roermond, March 8, 2013

This last miraculous event started at west beach and ended a day later in NYC with a very awesome ah-ha moment.

It involves Immaculee, a survivor of the Rwandan massacre who wrote a book called "Left to Tell," and Jessie, one of the children killed in the Newtown Massacre, and his mom.

I saw Immaculee give a retreat at My Father's House in Moodus, Connecticut, in 2010, and it was a powerful witness on the topic of forgiveness. Immaculee's entire family, mother, father, brother, sister, cousins, etc., were ALL slaughtered. She and two friends were hidden in a closet by a member of the tribe that was slaughtering people. The killers were in the house, and she remained silent praying the rosary as the tribe searched the house. She was so sure the killers were going find and kill her and her friends that she passed out. When they came to, the killers were gone.

The man sheltering them said that just as the killers started to turn the door knob to get into the room they were hiding in, one of the killers turned and said, "We trust you," and turned around and left, without opening the door to the room.

Years later, Immaculee wound up working at the United Nations, and the investigators of the massacre found the man who killed her entire family and brought him on his knees in front of her and told her, "Do whatever you want to him – kick him, spit on him, have us kill him." She said, "I forgive him."

These days, she still goes all over the world giving retreats to tell her story so that people learn how to forgive their enemies.

So, I'm on her mailing list, and two years ago she let me know that she was giving a retreat in NYC on thirty-third street at the Church of the Sacred Hearts of Mary and Jesus.

I booked the reservation, and weeks later I was in Stamford the day before staying with the friends who watch my dog when I travel, and I started to think, "I don't need to go to this retreat and hear the same thing again. I go to meetings every day. I know enough about forgiveness. I'll stay with my friends and have fun this weekend instead."

After making this decision, I went down to West Beach to meditate, but when I got there, I noticed a brand new children's playground blocking my view of the water where I usually park to meditate. It had a large picture of Jessie, one of the children who was killed at the Newtown Massacre, and a wax board that says "Loving, Nurturing, and Healing" on it. It was donated by the Angels Foundation.

I now remembered the story in the *Advocate* that I read about Jessie at the time of that horrible massacre and started crying. He was the child that had all the other kids hide in the closet, and in the story I read that December his older brother (8 years old) had told the mother of Jessie, "Don't worry, mom. In God's time, our whole lives are just a blink of his eyes and we will be with Jessie soon."

So, after this experience at the beach, I thought to myself, "I am going to go to the retreat now because maybe I don't know enough about forgiveness. If my son was killed, I don't think I could forgive the killer. Therefore, I'm going to Immaculee's retreat tomorrow."

The next morning, I took the train to NYC

and walked to 33rd Street still wondering if I did the right thing in coming or not. I arrived at the Church of the Sacred Heart of Jesus and Mary and went into the vestibule. I couldn't believe my eyes. There was a kneeler and a statue of St. Jude and St. Anthony right in front of me, and my eyes started tearing in Joy knowing I belonged at the retreat for sure now. I turned to a blonde lady who walked in behind me and said, "You're not going to believe this. I wasn't going to come today, and these are the two saints I petition to every day when I pray the rosary." She kindly said, "That's fine, but I don't know anything about that. I'm an Episcopalian." She came into the main church area with me following.

As soon as I got in, I went to speak with Immaculee. She remembered me from 7 years earlier, and I asked her if she thought the following locution was from Mary:

Lady of wisdom.

I wish to make you know how much you are loved. My eyes can see the contents of your heart.
I gaze upon my children all the time and know their every need.

My grace is sufficient to care for all your

needs.
I will never abandon my children that I received at the foot of my son's cross. You must stop looking to the world for consolation, for it gives none.
Take shelter in the wounds of my son and bask under the protection of my mantle.
Be grateful at all times for my son's suffering and your own.

Be powers of example by imitating my son and letting his light shine through you even while in distress.
When you are sinned against....
Remember my son's words on the cross. "Forgive them, Father. They know not what they do."
When you are tested .... PRAY
When you see a friend in need....
Respond with love AND service, not just words.
When you are persecuted,
Respond with an attitude of gratitude, and his grace will lead you home.

She said, "Definitely, Joe, that is our Lady speaking to you. Will you do me a favor? I'm doing something different at my retreats this year. Our lady appeared to the visionaries in Kebeho this year and told them, 'I desire that my children share their miracles.' Will you share your locution at the end of my presentation today?" I was now in awe and agreed to share.

So, Immaculee finished and called me up to the altar to share my locution in front of 500 or so attendees, and my miracle was well received. I sat down and the Episcopal woman who came in behind me went up to the Altar to give her witness. It was Jessie's mother sharing how she had forgiven her son's killer.

Now, I sat there in shock and awe of how God moves people when they resist the temptation to do their own thing. This event never would have happened if I had stayed with my friends in Stamford to have FUN. Awe beats FUN any day.

Well, I think this is a fitting place to stop sharing my miracles. These are only the 12 most significant miracles in my life. 12 is in my mind a very GOOD number, 12 apostles, 12 Steps in AA, 12 hours of light in a day.

Every day is a miracle, and so is every breath. YAHWEH = the beginning and the end.......

Prayers to St. Theresa. Photo by author.

SECTION 3: MY POETRY AND LOCUTIONS

Courtesy of Wikimedia. Old Saybrook Sunset. Photographer: Jeff Bellinger, September 15, 2014.

CRY SALVATION

Through the ancient desert trounced the silent winds of time.

Decades screaming for the light.

Caressing dreams of wandering souls.

Voices whispering in the sands of weathered beaches, on the shorelines of mankind.

Passionate trails of blighted past. Leading to the endless light.

Frightened not the faithful servants. Choosing good, instead of evil.

The fight is never all for naught.

Cry Oneness to the Lord.

Unity WILL overcome.

MIRACLE IN TIME

We are just a whisper. In the Miracle of Time.

What now, what hour, what day, what decade or what year.

We're sand grains in the moment, washed away with just a tear.

So, take a chance and laugh at life, Gods counted every hair.

Fall into Gods arms, be channels of his peace.

Were grains of sand at rest in the moment of His grace.

We are the children of a kind and gentle God. Who showers us with blessings every day.

Whose love has no conditions.

There are no strings attached.

So take a chance and laugh at life He's counted every hair.

Just fall into Gods arms of love.

Behold His Holy Face.

Surrounded with His Grace.

Courtesy of Wikimedia. Christ Pantocrator in the dome of the Church of the Holy Sepulchre, Old City of Jerusalem. Photographer, Andrew Shiva, May 13, 2014.

"Come follow me. I'll make the dark a merry waltz for thee."
Photo by author that inspired "In the Wilderness."

THE WILDERNESS

In the wilderness.

A single candle flickers.

In the dark and hardened heart of time.

It calls to us.

Come Follow me before the darkness overcomes the Light.

I call to YOU.

The path is narrow and the Way is true.

Come follow me.

I'll make the dark a merry waltz for thee.

Then you'll be mine.

And We'll dance together, through the end of time.

HEART OF MY HEART

Heart of my heart; Window of my Spirit.

Caress the Heavens with your eyes.

Forgiveness owes no penance now.

Forgiveness owes no penance now.

Follow Him through deep oceans of Peace, to warm shoulders of Love.

Courtesy of Wikimedia. Sacred Heart. All Saints Catholic Church, St. Peter's, MO. Photographer, Nheyob. July 8, 2014.

COMMUNION WITH A FRIEND

One sip of wine.

One bread in our time. One hope for mankind.

Who do you go to when dark days are near?

Now that the word of your day is fear.

Remember my mercy is ALWAYS near.

Revealed long ago by the spirit of Love.

The Lamb is alive and dancing a waltz, as the era of mercy follows His cross.

So wake up, and listen my kind hearted friends, Mercy yields forgiveness, but judgments offend.

So just stay with Him in your sacred place.

Just pray for mercy and receive His grace.

For His heart is as soft, as the breath of an angel.

He whispers His message in the still of His might.

Come and receive Him in the presence of light.

Come love your Jesus.

Come give up your fight!

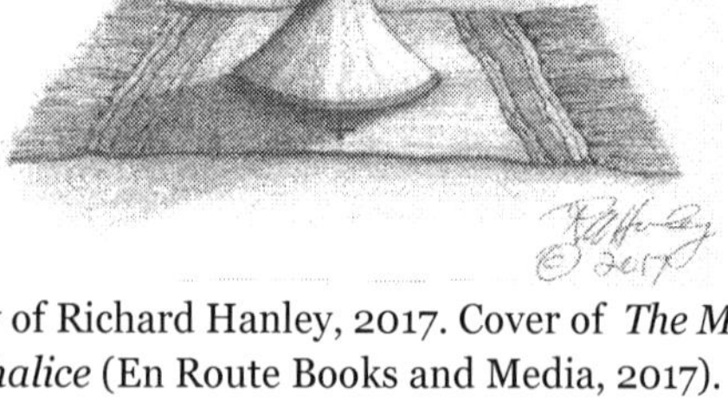

Courtesy of Richard Hanley, 2017. Cover of *The Missing Chalice* (En Route Books and Media, 2017).

ONE NATION OVER GOD

She was an Artist of the Heart.

She was a designer of Dreams.

She was a Believer in Hope and Love and all the Good things that life has to Bring.

She was a Whisper in a noisy World.

And a relief in a place of Despair and Hope.

She was a song in the Wind of time and a Poet in the melody of Life.

She was a designer of small things and of Large things alike.

She was never ruthless, rude, or impolite.

She was Great in so many ways that it spins the head to think,

What has become of her? Where has She

gone? What is Her next journey?

What Place is this without her Grace-Filled presence?

What Love is this without Her great support and Love?

What Generation is this that wastes away in the Wilderness!

What hope for those who choose Society over Spirituality?

What a bunch of lost souls in a Desert of Tumbleweed.

When will our Hope Return?

When will we get down on our Knees and Pray for Help?

When will we humble ourselves as our Fathers did?

When will we Love as our Mothers did?

When will we design, for ourselves, a life free of things, of this World, and bound to the

Principles of Spirituality that the God of our Fathers designed this country with?

When will Hope repair the Damage that Greed, Pride, and Lust have done?

In only a whisper, in only a moment, in only a sweet song, will our time be Done!

And to what avail is it?

To resist the Fight.

The Fight to save us, by the God Who made us.

Why do we run to the things that are Evil and from His grace-filled hands?

When will we ever remember the pains we have caused our-self?

"The fruit lies in the silence of our hearts," Pray for our country!

And when we look back and see the good things that he has done, in justice, to correct our Deeds!

Why don't we return to Him when dark days are here?

Now that the words of our day are Fear!

When the "Mist of Time" descends upon our worldly Thrones, When the wastefulness catches up with us,

Who will we go to? Who will we turn to?

When will we re-open Prayer in Schools?

When will we stop giving Government assistance to immoral acts and deeds?

When will we love our Country as much as our forefathers did?

Will we ever return to the Way we Were? Close to our God and far from our fears.

Turn off the Black Box that magnifies EVIL.

Turn around and open a good book or better yet open the good Book. Read to your Children! Read to your Families! Read to yourselves!

LEARN THE TRUTH

Start our crippled Country over Again!

With the principles of Love and Justice and Peace!

Liberty, YES, For ALL. But only with Justice for ALL;

And Only with time will our Wounds Heal.

We can't make a thing happen!

We must REPENT – and - LET THINGS HAPPEN.

Then our Lady of Victory will return!!!

GRACE

Before the dawn of time. There was Grace.

Grace marked time and watched over creation.

Grace gave wings to hope and Eagles soared upon her winds.

She was a light in the wilderness and a sound in the silent word.

As father time whispered, grace amplified his words and turned them into good actions.

When the son of God was born, grace carried him throughout his journey.

When he died, she carried him home. Likewise, she will Carry us, if we let her.

Grace moves people without touching them and touches people without moving them.

She has as many children as the stars in the sky and the sands in the seas.

What a great name to bear!

Thank you, Grace.

Courtesy of Wikimedia. Gustave Doré Illustration of St. Lucia carrying Dante to the Gates of Purgatory, which is the entrance to Paradise.

ONE FAMILY

Love has revealed to you the silence of his nature today.

He is one.

There is only one.

We are one.

We are one Holy Spirit.

When we have hope, wisdom will come.

He will triumph over all. We are one we are one.

Answer the call.

No deed is too small.

The fruit lies in the silence of our heart.

AT MEMPKIN MONASTERY

I met the flickering candle in the wilderness of mankind.

Today he taught me the lessons of love and peaceful mind.

At Mempkin Trappist Monastery the river of life runs gently on my mind.

Disturbed only by an occasional noisy mosquito.

Or, the report of a sunning rattler by another Bethesda retired brother monk.

Here where world peace is prayed for with earnest devotion.

Even the rattlers make no noise.

I wonder if the brothers tamed them.

The Jordan River.

RIVER OF LIFE LOCUTION

When Your well is full of me it is time to let it flow out to others.

If you try to keep yourself full, you will lose what you have, for I am the river of life.

No well is deep enough to contain the abundance of my mercy.

To those I give much too much is expected of. Be not like the Dead Sea full of riches and minerals but not flowing out.

Be instead like the river Jordan living water flowing in and out feeding the poor and the hungry.

Irrigating and creating rich soil on its banks for the sower of good seeds.

Growing into abundant fields of the master's crop - prepared fully for the harvest.

HERE OR THERE RIDDLE

The more we listen the less we hear.

The less we hear the more we understand.

The more we understand, the less we are.

The less we are, the closer we are.

The closer we are, the harder it gets.

The harder it gets, the closer we are.

Only when here can we die to self.

When we die to self, we are no longer here.

No longer here, is Heaven.

HEAVEN ON EARTH

I sit in stillness. At first the noise is too much to bear, as the thoughts of the flesh fight to stay and be recognized.

Then, in creep the sweet tiny soft thoughts, ever so patient and graceful. The storm finally begins to calm as wisdom nudges insanity out of the way.

Mercifully, justice edges out liberty and peace triumphs over war.

As fright surrenders to faithfulness, the battle begins to turn, and I become freed into an ocean of mercy and love.

Finally, silence triumphs and time stands still as in eternity.

When here, I bask in the silent, motionless, unconditional love and warmth of the son, in a sweet taste of heaven on earth.

SONG IN THE HEART

I have a song in my heart and the song in my heart is the Lord of the dance.

And the song said - be still and know that I am yours.

I'm the whisper in the wind, and the sparkle in your eyes. The mystery that lives forever in the kingdom in your mind.

I weep when you weep and sing when you sing.

In the winds of time the secret is revealed. In the fulness of time I will save you all.

I will take all your tears and dry them in the wind driven rains of my grace.

My peace will be with you, Now and at the end of time, I will never abandon you.

I am the Lord of the dance enjoy the Music.

A NEW CREATION

Love embarks on a new journey as the sorrow of man surrenders to the mercy of the river of life.

Which flows slowly out of mountain lakes to oceans of peace.

Summits of the tallest achievements of man have fallen to streams of divine intervention.

Which slowly erode man's hungry passion for false pride, greed, and lust.

The creator of true wealth has grown a forest of fruit bearing trees, in the middle of a desert full of tumble weed, fruitless vegetation, and fool's gold.

SERENITY OF NATURE

Slide gently into an ocean breeze with the sun setting reluctantly into a horizon of hope.

Faithfully practicing the surrendering of time to effortless sleep. Soundly awakening stars glittering in dark Sky with promising dawns.

Sparkles of sunbeams with twinkling eyes and glistening souls beaming in the twilight of our life.

Gifted with giant soft hearts of gold shining in our shadows.

Filled with spiritual energy and feeding on our powerless strength.

Fearless in decisions frightened only of losing what they see as theirs.

Praying foolishly that their past won't become the future of our loved ones.

LAKESIDE DINER

At the window by lake side sat three new friends of different nations.

Marveling at the murky water.

Joyful from the masters work.

Broken often but not destroyed.

Awakened by the pain of love.

Crippled by a wonderful truth, that freedom will cause many crosses.

Destined to be friends forever as nations crumble to and fro.

Searching for that awesome light and the endless peace it causes Finally - of peace - and formed by Love.

THE SINGLE MAN

A single man sat quietly on the point of time, at the intersection of eternity.

The winds howled to his right and left, Beams of broken sun pierced and penetrated his stilled heart.

Awakened at last his heart danced as the winds blew so hard that the angry seas flattened in front of his eyes.

A clear blue area of sky above slowly surrendered to a circle of majestically hovering clouds that appeared angrily out of nowhere.

Then as he remained quiet, On the point, the winds asked, What is the secret of time?

As they blew ever more intently, he humbly answered. I know not the answer for in the Creator's encyclopedia of eternity there is only reference to love and time is not even in the bibliography!

ALONE

Alone no more.

No rest for your soul.

No dreams left to chase.

No pain left unexplored.

No rules left to break.

No mountains left to shake.

Just Follow your heart,

His days are soon to come.

The era of peace is near fear not.

I am in you, and will work through you.

Let my light shine upon all in your path.

Remember always how much He loves you.

IN THE SON

When in silence I listen into peace I am born.

The time of our Lord the era of peace.

The son of the father to us is born the way, the truth, and the light.

From a distant place of light and peace the son of the father comes to his flock.

In pastures of green, his love can be seen, He makes us all witness to his great dream.

Love of the father and a peace of the son the hope of the Spirit three in one.

Come answer his call no deed is too small; come lay in the pasture and bask in the Son.

STATE OF THE WORLD

Flying high the wicked ways of the world.

Destroying all on impact.

While innocence crashes, Evil smiles and justice frowns.

Liberty and justice for all has become liberty or justice for none – pick your poison.

Peace smiles at chaos knowing it will eventually prevail.

For all is necessary for the human condition.

And both evil and good seasons all for eternal bliss.

As the moon bleeds sorrow and the earth quakes.

The hands of time strike midnight as the

sun awaits a new dawn.

Will mankind awake or continue its self-induced coma.

Only time will tell a soul.

Then peace and justice will prevail .....

Courtesy of Wikimedia. Banknote vignette with female figures representing Liberty and Justice. Artist, Asher Brown Durand, Circa 1824-1837.

SPIRIT DRIVEN

Light, energy, pulsating waves of the Joy of creation.

Made by a sweep of the master's hand.

Fond thoughts of the Father's mind.

Breathed into life.

Formed from cosmic dust into beaconing eyes and beating hearts.

Never understanding or finding, but always seeking, the meaning of Life....

MY PINK CLOUD

As the soft continuous rain on the roof caresses my soul, it enlightens my heart, I envision an ocean of mercy.

My eyes tear ....

As a feeling of bliss enters into the moment. I become heavy yet light simultaneously.

In this frozen piece of time, I realize that in my unknowing, all reference to time and place disappear, as mercy speaks, using the sacred silent language that exists in the space between words.

As my body mind and spirit surrender and become one with the mystery that occupies everything, everywhere, and everybody.

I disappear into heavenly nothingness, coming into complete conscious contact with the OTHER; AKA DEATH, of the False self...

GRATITUDE

Finding the sun behind every cloud.

Seeing the smile behind a frown.

Loving without conditions.

Living each day with joy.

Knowing that life will never end, Yet living each day like it's the end.

Forgetting the past and ignoring the future.

Praying for peace and accepting chaos.

Chasing rainbows in thunder storms.

Gently riding the roller coaster called life.

For time is short but love is long -

All of life is a happy song, and when we stop fighting....... LOVE is born.

TO THE CHILDREN OF LIGHT

Move on my children of light.

Tell the world to pray for days of peace and love.

He who is with you forever needs you to come to his heart today.

Too long has he borne the world's weight on his intercessions alone.

He needs all his brothers and sisters to pray for peace and accept his mercy.

It is a time for all to accept his mercy and know him as their only savior; there is no other.

Move with diligence to help others learn the word and accept the sacraments of penance and the Eucharist.

Repent and forgive all so that you may be

forgiven.

Pray the rosary and do the mercy chaplet daily.

Help all who are in your path on a daily basis, pray more, fast more.

Forgive more easily those who trespass.

Moving diligently the clouds of fate, His time is soon to come.

Watch the sky for signs.

The spirit will show the way to the children of light.

Peace be with you, be not afraid or worried.

MARY'S WORD LOCUTION 7/5/2016

In the stillness of your heart, my son will come in the cloud of unknowing.

He will bathe you in the blood of the innocent slaughter.

He will drown your sorrows and wash away your tears.

His heart still bleeds for all mankind.

He needs trusted servants to help him quench the fires of hell on earth.

Listen carefully, pray frequently for the era of peace.

Tell my children I desire that they share their miracles.

Be not afraid be aware and in awe of his mercy.

His day is soon to come.

His mercy will endure forever.

My children will be saved.

His Church will be repaired and exonerated and start loving and feeding the poor and hungry again, regardless of their religion.

His love surpasses all human understanding.

Stay strong in prayer and contemplative silence daily.

You are loved beyond your wildest dreams.

Peace be with you.

OUR LADY OF WISDOM

I wish to make you know how much you are loved.

My eyes can see the contents of your heart.

I gaze upon my children all the time and know their every need.

My grace is sufficient to care for all your needs.

I will never abandon my children that I received at the foot of my son's cross.

You must stop looking to the world for consolation for it gives none.

Take shelter in the wounds of my son, and bask under the protection of my mantle.

Be grateful at all times for my son's suffering and your own.

Be powers of example, by imitating my son and letting his light shine through you, even while in distress.

When you are sinned against....

Remember my sons words on the cross.

"Forgive them, father. They know not what they do."

When you are tested ....

PRAY.

When you see a friend in need....

Respond with love AND service not just words.

When you are persecuted, respond with an attitude of gratitude.

My son's grace will lead you home.

ERA OF MERCY

The time is here. The way is clear.

Mercy will uproot fear.

Mayhem will disappear. Believe and be saved!

The end of one time will be the beginning of a new time.

The faith of few will save the souls of many.

Horror and tears will be replaced with ecstasy and joy.

Stand fast in your faith and ignore what you see with worldly eyes.

My love and mercy surpasses all human understanding.

My ways are incomprehensible to the human mind.

Open your mind and heart to me, and I will set you free.

Surrender your will to me, and I will work many miracles through you.

You will become a light in dark days, and a beacon of hope.

Surrender and acceptance are now critical, not optional.

Peace be with you.

Love and service is the key.

MY CHILDREN

The Body of Christ is as strong as it ever was.

Do not allow the media, who magnify the lies, distort your picture of the Truth, who is now and ever will be.

We are one body in the mystery of the cross.

Fear not the state of the world as reported by the father of lies.

We are one, we are one, we are one body, one blood, in Christ Jesus.

The true head of the Church cannot be destroyed by anything of this world, and neither can his body be removed from its Head.

Do not allow my children's minds to be destroyed by lies.

If you are truthful with them about me -

how can you allow them to be constantly subjected to lies and non-reality?

Bring your children back to me.

Remove the poison apple from your homes.

Your children need their souls washed, not their brains.

Who chooses the channels in your home?

Children’s bread is fatal when parents fail to stop it from being fed to their sons and daughters.

Who are your children's idols? Who used to be???

Wake up and do the right thing for your family!

Turn off your tele(distant)vision for two weeks and Read the truth to your charges instead.

The truth is not distant, but the world is making it look that way.

Don't let tv watch your children for you. They deserve reality, not tv's version of it!

There is no tv in heaven, but there is constant vision of truth through love.

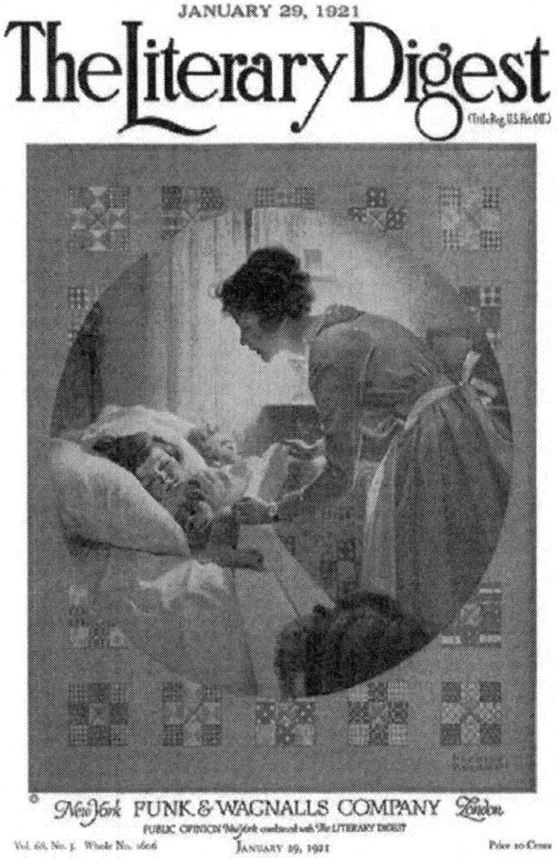

Courtesy of Wikimedia. Norman Rockwell's *Mother Tucking Children in Bed* appeared on the cover of The Literary Digest published 20-Jan-1921.

ONE

We are one holy family we are one. Son, mother, and the other one.

Mother Earth, sister sun and the moon.

Blood of Christ seat of wisdom and the womb.

Holy, holy, holy three in one.

Love peace and justice all in one.

Forgiveness leads to peace for everyone.

Forgiveness leads to peace for everyone.

Come into his presence see his face. Come into his presence every one.

Then you'll know the secret of the son.

He'll hide you in his wounds until he comes.

He'll be with you forever when he comes.

You'll soon be saints in heaven with the Son.

You'll be at peace forever in the sun.

Forever in the light, all will be one.

Courtesy of Wikimedia. Artist, Jan Siberechts, Saint Francis Preaching to the Animals, 1666.

SILENT WORD OF GOLD

Silence will deafen the chaos as the era of peace shatters all resistance.

Speak not listen carefully as grace replaces waste.

As wisdom overcomes insanity.

As the mighty fall and the weak rise.

Peace will prevail and mercy will triumph!

Then you will be my people, and I will be your God!

HEART OF GOLD

Heart of my heart, window of my spirit. You are the way the light and the truth.

Now is the time, this is the hour the moment the day that he has made.

Take up his cross and spread the good news that He is Lord today.

We pass this way but once today to live and love and pray.

We wait for God - the Holy Spirit - to bless each precious day.

Our life is graced with many gifts to pass our brothers way.

The flow of love must never end lest we shall wilt away. So, may I always seek and follow God.

Thy will be done not mine!!!

THE SPIRIT OF CHRIST

We are one – there is no separation.

I am in you and you are in me we are one!

Unity has overcome; some just don't accept that.

Your experiences are my experiences, your love is my love, your failures are my failures, your life is my life, your words are my words, your sorrows are my sorrows, and when your will is my will you're in heaven already!

Heaven is a state of mind, not a location.

You are a part of me, only your mind can pretend that is not true because of my gift of free will.

ALZHEIMER'S THE GIFT?

I am beginning to think that Alzheimer's is a gift to the bearer of the disease. Mom is an amazing woman. She's in heaven now with the other Saints. In her late life, she suffered much, but in her Creator's great mercy, she remembered nothing.

After years of selfless service from her, her family likewise benefited by being forced to be selfless servants as caregivers to her. Gratitude to serve was not required but highly recommended to those attending her demented mind and failing body.

The constant cry of "how could God do this to her?" was really a cry of "how could God do this to us?" There was mercy for her in her disease.

As mom was already in a state of involuntary, mindless, knowledge less, heavenly bliss.

Thank God?

LOVE IS THE WINDOW TO KNOWING ME

Love is the window to knowing me; without it nobody can see my face.

My heart is full of sorrow for those who never learn the power of Love.

Love accepts all and is perfect in forgiveness; To forget oneself is to love oneself.

To love all is to love me, for I am love - and to be in Love is to be in me. Come now into my heart and know the true meaning of divine love.

In the moment, love can become perfect in silence of one's mind.

Thoughtless is fullness, in the cloud of unknowing is found pure love.

I am pure love.

How great is the love found in total surrender to my will.

He who contemplates my word day and night is with you forever.

His love is inexhaustible and almighty.

His mercy endures forever.

Fear no man!

Remember always the truth written about Mary and Martha.

I am allowed to favor, and I have favorites.

I am not accountable to the ACLU.

I pick and choose whom I favor.

I came and got the people who think they came and got me.

Thinking is a human problem - contemplation is a remedy for that.

Love is the key to salvation, start with me, then everything else will come freely.

TRIBAL CONQUISTADORS

My friends in the spirit have something much bigger than anything the world can bring them.

They hang out in tribes and share their experiences in life.

God is life; God takes our darkness and makes it light on us and all those around us; We call this grace.

It allows us to face and walk through fear and pain.

To live each day like it's our last.

To love without conditions!

To speak kindly and without fear.

To surrender quickly and to forgive immediately those who harm us.

To walk a steady beam without worry of falling or failing.

To get out of our own way and let God's light shine through us even while in distress.

To love and serve each other, being the eyes and hands of our co-creator.

To share God's pain and joy by relentlessly accepting the struggle we call life.

One day at a time anything is possible; then we learn how to live in the moment where everything is awesome.

Where love finally triumphs over fear.

In a place called the eternal now, aka heaven on earth.

COME INTO THE LIGHT - THE NARROW GATE

Come, fear no more.

My love is here. My time has come. My ways will save. My wounds will heal.

My light will shine.

Listen and learn. Act and be saved.

Now is the time! Here is the daylight!

No more is the pain. No more is the grief. My mercy endures!

My love overcomes! My tears wash your souls! My eyes see your needs.

Surrender today. Give me your all! Answer the call! No deed is too small! I love you all!

Follow the light. The dark will fall.

A PART OF GOD?

I've tried to better understand the un-understandable mystery of God.

I believe today that we are all a part of God - unless we THINK we are not a part of GOD.

But even when we think we are apart from GOD - we are still a part of GOD.

We are God's skin.

When we get out of the way, God works through us.

Perfect humility is total absence of self - and that's impossible until I die.

BECAUSE, as I learned in Baltimore catechism at age 7.

But now, I believe it to be true---

"God IS EVERYWHERE, GOD IS EVERY-

ONE, GOD IS EVERYTHING".

EVERY ONE IS a part GOD.

EVERYTHING IS part of GOD.

EVERYWHERE IS part of GOD.

GOD COMES TO US DISGUISED AS OUR LIFE!

Where is God?

We think God is in us and works through us, but have we ever considered we are a part of God?

God is everywhere,

God is everything – and that looking for God – is like a dog chasing its tail.

The only thing that can separate us from God is the gift/curse of free will.

LETTER TO GOD

I feel that peace and stillness now, and I know that is you. You are the stillness in my heart, that only enters into my consciousness when I am willing to let it enter my mind, which is usually chaotic.

The key to the door between my heart and mind can only be opened with the key of willingness. That willingness happens when I sit in silence and contemplate your love and mercy.

When I stop attaching to my thoughts, and surrender to your silent words. When I feel you gaze upon me - with unconditional approval. When I start to understand that this is your body, not mine, and that what I don't know is vastly more important than what I think I know.

Then, in an unexpected flash of hope, I suddenly, for a joyous microsecond, understand, with my heart only, a new truth.

That you are in me, that I am in you, that WE are ONE. That the only thing that can separate me from you is free will and that that gift that you also experienced on earth is an irrevocable free gift/curse from the Father.

It's a gift if I use it to seek you, and a curse if I use it to seek myself. It's a gift if I use it to serve others, and a curse if I use it to serve myself. It's a gift if I love and accept others unconditionally, and a curse if used conditionally.

It's so hard though, Lord, to act on what I know is true. To love my enemies. To love the people who hurt me.

To forgive the people who kill me, as you did. To accept dying for my brothers and sisters.

Thank you for this time with you today!

With hope and gratitude, your brother, friend, and Lover.

Joe

GOD'S RESPONSE TO TRUSTED SERVANTS

We are pleased with the offerings you've been making.

Listen carefully; speak even more carefully.

Silence is frequently the best response. Waste not time trying to figure things out. Think and act on the desires of the heart - not the mind.

Place your trust in Jesus, and your life will be beyond your wildest dreams.

Stay focused on living a humble life of love and service. Act only on what is directly in front of you.

Be patient and persistent in your silent time each morning. More will be revealed as needed.

Your Brother, Friend and Lover - GOD

NEW JOURNEY

Love embarks on a new journey - as the sorrow of man surrenders to the mercy of the river of life.

Which flows slowly out of mountain lakes to oceans of peace.

Summits of the tallest achievements of man have fallen to streams of divine intervention.

Which slowly erodes man's hungry passion for false pride and greed.

The creator of true wealth has grown a forest of fruit bearing trees.

In the middle of a desert full of tumble weed and fruitless vegetation and fool's gold.

DAY OF MERCY ON THE HUDSON

Red clusters - wild yet dainty quivering in an autumn breeze. Lighthearted children surrounded by laughing wind and talking trees. Listless waters wait, as ripples start to stir.

Memories of days gone by.

Sweetened by the revival of mercy and light in the sky. A flight of non-believers whisked to eternal wisdom of the spirit.

A day of mercy and myrrh within a city of doom and gloom. Prophets of doom and gloom convert for a day to spread joy and truth.

Will tomorrow return to science and fiction. The black box of man's judgement was human for the hour of mercy on Thursday at 3 on flight 153.

As gratitude conquered fear in a day of mercy and hope on the Hudson.

Original painting of the Divine Mercy (by Eugeniusz Kazimirowski in 1934). This is the only painting which was done under the indications of Sister Faustina when she was still alive, unlike the painting by Adolf Hyła which was done in 1943 after Saint Faustina's death in 1938 but still the most known.

MIGHTY LOVE

(What God says to us every time we get our own thoughts out of the way.)

My beloved child. Mighty is my love for you.

Full of mercy, hope, and grace. Before the dawn of time I knew you.

Your voice is music to my ears. When I gaze upon you I see myself.

Everything you do pleases me immensely.

I call to you. I thirst for you. I bleed for you. I died for you.

I feel your pains. I share your gains. I'm here for you.

Now and forever. Nothing can separate us except your will.

Accept me! Please don't leave me again!

FORGIVENESS

I must forgive everyone who hurt me including myself, not the old damaged self, the self-reborn in Christ Jesus.

My old small story reveals who I was, why I was ill, and who put me there.

My new story, the big eternal story is who saved me, who I am being saved from, and what do we do to keep me saved.

My illness is just a part of my salvation story, which I must share with others in order to stay saved.

It is atonement for my sins.

Only God can use our sins to save us!

COME LISTEN TO THE SILENCE

Into the chaos of mankind creeps the wisdom of God's Love.

The master of strife and hope.

Listen carefully without ears to the word that makes no sound in the silent chambers of your heart.

Pay no attention to the chatter of the World.

Courtesy of Wikimedia. Holy Silence Icon of the Old Believers. Circa, 19th Century.

MY MERCY FREEDOM PRAYER-POEM

In the wilderness a single candle flickers, in the dark and hardened heart of time.

Left by a traveler from a distant place of light and hope.

Discovered by the faith of many trusting souls, inspired by one spirit of Love.

Guided by the breath of singing breezes, dancing in a flash of light.

Overflowing from the source of all mercy love and time - on the battlefield of life in the kingdom of our mind.

Free me, oh Lord, from the numbness of addiction and all that separates me from a total awareness of your love and mercy.

Make me dependent only on your mercy that endures forever.

Save me from the self-centered fear that looks to destroy the relationship I need with you.

Calm me and surround me with the peace of your love - bind me to your love - first and then to all my brothers and sisters in oneness with your Holy Spirit.

Awaken, in me, the hope of an everlasting union with you.

Separate me from all things of the world that lure and attract me away from you.

Remove from me the thoughts of past bitterness and resentments that distracted me from your truth.

Implant in me an everlasting desire to love and serve my brothers and sisters.

Help me to accept, with gratitude, all the situations you place in front of me.

Amen

REGAINING PEACE

The eternal journey from the head to the heart.

The inner quest for the inner quiet.

The immortal diamond buried deep within the suffering soul.

The reality that lives within the lie and awakens only after free will is surrendered voluntarily.

Then ever so gently the light begins to overcome the darkness.

By revealing layer after layer of the old self until it is imprisoned and then the Son is released and begins to shine brightly through us again.

Then peace finally is resurrected within us.

Then we become - Dust in the wind!

ENCHANTED RIVERS OF LIFE

Sky widening, embracing dreams of hope.

Coloring horizons and bridging worlds of wonderment.

Clouds embracing colorful circles of ever cascading light.

Fountains of bewilderment and pain restored as one love.

Floating on a calm enchanted river widening to an pool of joy.

In an enchanted wilderness created by our spirit guide.

Cry oneness, but carefully accept a universal bond with humanity.

UNIVERSAL FACES OF GOD

People used to believe there is a star for every person on earth.

But now science has proved there are approximately seventy galaxies for each person on earth.

If we could understand from this – completely – how small we are and how great our God is – we would have perfect humility.

After a share in my 12-step meeting on the topic of how dangerous it is to compare and feel differently, I started brainstorming about differences.

I came up with this:

If I could leave my body and go through that tunnel, with bright light at the end, that my father described when he had his cardiac arrest in 1972, after he was successfully resuscitated, and if I was allowed to look back at the entire present universe through God's eyes NOW.

I would see a gigantic living mosaic comprised of every man woman child, creature, and object in the universe.

I would See, through spiritual eyes, that God made everything DIFFERENT so it would fit together better. Like a giant beautiful living quilt our spiritual mother could have knitted.

And then viewing this miracle, in that precise moment, I would be ready to enter the womb of salvation and be in God's light - where hell would be only a distant, fleeting, negative thought.

And my heart would understand that I was now viewing – the faces and skin of my God, and what a tiny piece of that I am.

I would instantly know that God is not up there; He is in fact in me.

And that every living creature is a piece of God in action because God is s verb not a noun. And we are each part of God, unless we use our free will to separate ourselves from Him.

GOD'S HOPE FOR US LOCUTION

"My hope for you my children is that you will share about your journey with me to conversion so that others may heal by getting hope.

I desire that my people share their lives openly as my apostles did during and after my death.

They went in pairs and teams and gave away what they had so freely been given and witnessed, all their miracles and mine.

They converted the world in early Christianity by sharing with each other and being one family.

They sought nothing in return and lived in tents as I did, and received everything they needed.

They had supper with each other every day

and shared their lives openly and prayed together at the end of each day for healing for themselves and others. Just like we did at the Last Supper.

What has happened? Where is that fellowship and communion now? Tell my people that's what I want NOW. For families and friends to do every night.

Turn off all electronics and have dinner together at table. Share their day with each other, come into communion, like we did at the Last Supper.

When you share your stories with each other, you are sharing me, for I am life, and when you talk about your own life, you're sharing me, and it increases the strength of my mystical body.

I am everything, I am everywhere, I am everyone. I am life. There is no other. If you don't go to worship, that's ok because my father and I never desired the building of temples or churches.

We desired the building of communion like at the Last Supper, of families because God is a family.

Remember this scripture. I will write my commandments in their hearts, and they will need no other teachers and I will be their God and they will be my people.

I entered human form to show you how to live and how to die, serving your brothers and sisters by staying close to sinners and the poor and hungry. Being willing to die for your brothers and sisters.

I walked in the wilderness with my disciples SHOWING people how to live the word. Like I had St Francis do; he knew what I wanted. He died naked in the arms of two brothers who laid him on the earth. He taught his brothers to preach the gospel at all times and when necessary use words.

I never asked for temples and churches to be erected in my name. You are my temples!

Go back to the historic ways of the body of Christ. You are all part of the body of Christ; start acting like it.

Love your Jesus; don't worship me. Imitate me; that's all I desire ...."

WHISPERS OF TWILIGHT

In the silence of the evening, mist arises hope of everlasting joy. As the evening precedes the dawn so the master dispenses time.

Everlasting whispers connect precious breaths of life. His mercy is forever blossoming in those who reject their own desires.

Procreating humble humans with divine love for their brothers and sisters. Sons and daughters of mercy defending all that is of GOD.

Always waiting for the dawn, listening to the whispers of time. One heart, one mind, one love for all mankind.

Bathed in the rays of the Son's everlasting salvation and Love.

Cryoneness - His blood has reversed all sin!

Believe and be saved! He is and we are!

LORD OF THE DANCE

I have a song in my heart, and the song in my heart is the Lord of the dance.

And the song said, “Be still and know that I am yours.”

I'm the whisper in the wind and the sparkle in your eyes. The mystery that lives forever in the kingdom of your mind.

I weep when you weep and sing when you sing.

In the winds of time, the secret is revealed. In the fulness of time, I will save you all.

I will take all your tears and dry them in the wind driven rains of my grace.

My peace will be with you, Now and at the end of time; I will never abandon you.

I am the Lord of the dance; enjoy the Music.

AT DUSK

Set your sails for a new destination.

Joyful bursts of life hide behind every cloud.

The perfume of roses and wine fills the horizon.

Place yourself at his disposal completely – half-way is not enough.

Stop regretting the past; stay in the moment of peace and love.

You are in my heart and I in yours.

I have great plans for you and all my children.

Plans with an everlasting future of peace and love enlightened by the countenance of his holy face.

Illuminated with a brightness greater than the sun.

Will be your calling when fully revealed to you.

Taste and see the goodness of his love, one day at a time.

Don't quit before the miracle(s) happens.

Peace be with you!

Courtesy of Wikipedia. Lone Sailboat at Dusk. Photographer, Daniel Ramirez, November 26, 2010.

NO MORE TEARS

I will take all your tears and make them like drops of water in the wind driven rains of my Grace.

The oceans of the world do not contain enough force within them to drive one of my chosen from Me.

The tides of time and turbulence will only increase the devotion from my children of Light.

During this Lenten season, man's awareness of my presence will increase one-hundred fold.

My Holy Face will cease to be defiled within this generation.

Peace, Love, and Mercy will overcome jealousy, greed, and pride.

Nations will fall and walls of resistance will crumble.

As the era of Peace is ushered in, the faith of few will save the souls of many. My Church will be exonerated and convert the nations.

Flee all that is evil, and turn your hearts over to me. For I am patient and kind of heart. Pray without ceasing for the era of peace.

Love is the key to my kingdom.

Courtesy of Wikimedia.
Artist, Jusepe de Ribera, Circa 1612-13.

THE PARADOX OF LIFE

Love forgets what somebody did to me, but anger remembers.

Love creates people; lust destroys people.

When Love endures, hate ends.

When Love never ends, hate never starts.

Sin is the beginning of hell and the end of heaven.

Wisdom is the end of knowing and the beginning of believing.

Doubt is the start of hopelessness and the end of trust.

Powerlessness starts with willingness and ends with surrender.

Sobriety starts with surrender and ends with surrender.

When I forget myself, I remember who I am.

When I love MY SELF - I hate the world.

Faith will save what fear has stolen.

The souls of many will be saved by the faith of a few.

When Love arrives, fear departs.

There can be no unity without love.

The hearts of the restless defy the peace of God; peace will come to those who learn how to love.

Do not defy your higher power with lies; embrace it with truth.

Fear will disappear when love appears.

Hope will strengthen what doubt has weakened.

Serenity will replace chaos with good orderly direction.

PRESS FORWARD LOCUTION

I will be the wind at your back and the hand on your shoulder.

The joy that dries your tears and lifts your heart.

The way in the wilderness and the light in the distance.

The comforter of your afflictions and the lamp at your feet.

The just will love you, and the wicked will fear you.

The mighty will fall, and the weak will triumph.

The way of truth will overcome the greed of the world.

And the lion will dance with the lamb as the era of mercy enters time.

SURRENDERING IS BELIEVING

I can't believe in God if I can't believe in myself.

Therefore I believed in "nothing."

And "nothing" (my false self) was my problem.

I was wired in reverse; because I didn't believe in a higher power, God was nothing and so was I.

So if I drank nothing to death, it didn't matter to the person I had become.

There were no consequences.

Now I believe in God!

I am part of that God, and that God is a part of me, not apart from me.

Thanks to the 12 steps.

I communicate with that God, every day, and at times I'm in constant conscious contact with my higher power.

I have found that listening to my God means listening to other people and my true self, in that order.

And I take all the thoughts I need and leave the rest because resentments (mine and other people's) are like stray cats.

If I don't feed them, they will go away.

Joe Avalos and Richard Rohr. Photo provided by the author.

TRUSTING THE MOMENT

I CLOSE MY EYES AND OPENED MY HEART.

I FEEL THE BREEZE GENTLY CARESS MY FACE ARMS AND LEGS. THE BREATH OF THE SPIRIT HOLDS ME IN SILENT CHILDLIKE AWE.

THE TREES WHISPER A SOFT LOVE SONG AS THE AWARENESS OF THEIR PRESENCE ENTERS.

THE AUGUST GREEN LEAVES ARE DANCING IN THE WIND AS MY EYES OPEN.

I MUSE, WHERE IS THIS WIND COMING FROM AND TO WHERE WILL IT RETURN?

MY SALVATION PHILOSOPHY

1) SURRENDER
2) PARTICIPATE
3) DEMONSTRATE

First Salvation is not being home. Then, salvation is coming home. Then, salvation is BEING home.

--

First becoming apart from the whole. Then becoming a part of the whole. Then becoming one with the whole.

--

1) Receiving the call
2) Hearing the call
3) Being the CALL

SET SAIL LOCUTION

Set your sails for a new destination. Joyful bursts of life hide behind every cloud. The perfume of roses and wine fill the horizon.

Place yourself at his disposal completely – half-way is not enough. Stop regretting the past; stay in the moment with peace and love.

You are in my heart, and I in yours. I have great plans for you and all my children.

Plans with an everlasting future of peace and love lightened by the countenance of the Holy Face.

Illuminated with a brightness greater than the sun. Will be your calling when fully revealed to you.

Taste and see the goodness of his love one day at a time. Don't quit before the miracle happens. Be at peace; His peace is with you now.

SHOW ME YOUR WILL PRAYER/POEM

Now is the time; this is the hour the moment the day that he has made.

Take up your cross and spread the good word that he is Lord today.

Oh, Holy Spirit, beloved of my soul, I adore you.

Enlighten me, guide me, strengthen me, console me.

Tell me what I should do; give me Your orders.

I promise to submit myself to all that You desire of me and to accept all that You permit to happen to me.

Let me only know Your will.

THE CRUCIFIXION

The moon bled, and the earth quaked, as time entered quietly into the era of mercy.

Man's passions surrendered to the shadow of the earth against the celestial body of Love.

The blameless stars of distant galaxies danced as Mercy conquered Judgement.

A fitting End for now.

More will be revealed.

More poems, locutions, and miracles will be added to my Website as they happen. Go to cryoness.com to share your story, your miracles, your poems, and your music on one of my social media groups NOW.

Or

Download the app from the App Store or Google Play and Listen to WCAT Internet

Radio. Every Wednesday at 8PM Eastern Time. You may also go to http://www.wcatradio.com and click “Listen Now” at the top of the page to a live show.

Call in! Or, simply listen to my recordings – over a year’s worth of wisdom from the Holy Face is posted on there already.

http://www.wcatradio.com/cryoneness

The Word of God needs New, New testaments that prove God and God’s Mercy IS alive, well, and working through His people NOW. Thanks for reading my writings and witnesses.

AND

Don’t quit before YOUR Miracle(s) Happen.

Bye for now,

Your Brother Joe A. and my dog “Mercy” - assistant poet whom I picked up on Divine Mercy Sunday 2012.

JOSEPH AVALOS
HTTP://WWW.CRYONENESS.ORG

JOE'S DOG, MERCY

91752406R00111

Made in the USA
Middletown, DE
07 October 2018